Believe in Love : Coloring book

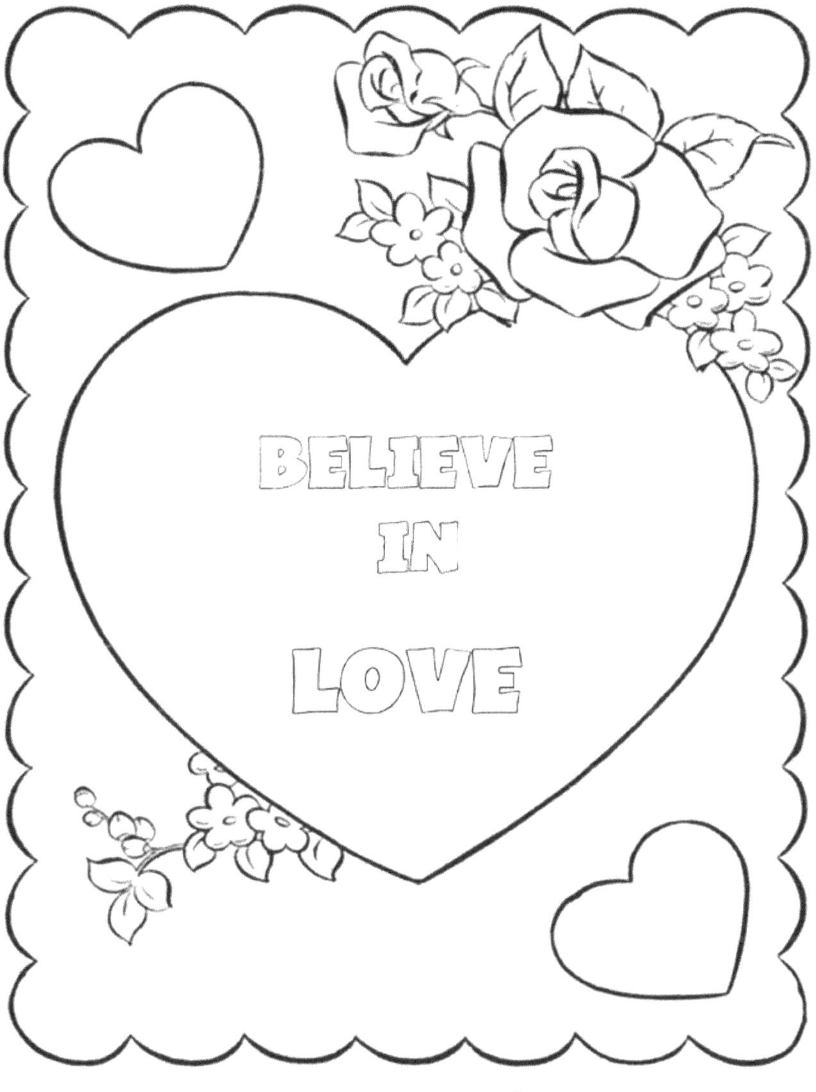

Nina Packer

Believe in Love : Doddle Coloring book

Copyright: Published in the United States by Nina Packer
Published January 2018

ISBN-13: 978-1983707773

ISBN-10: 1983707775

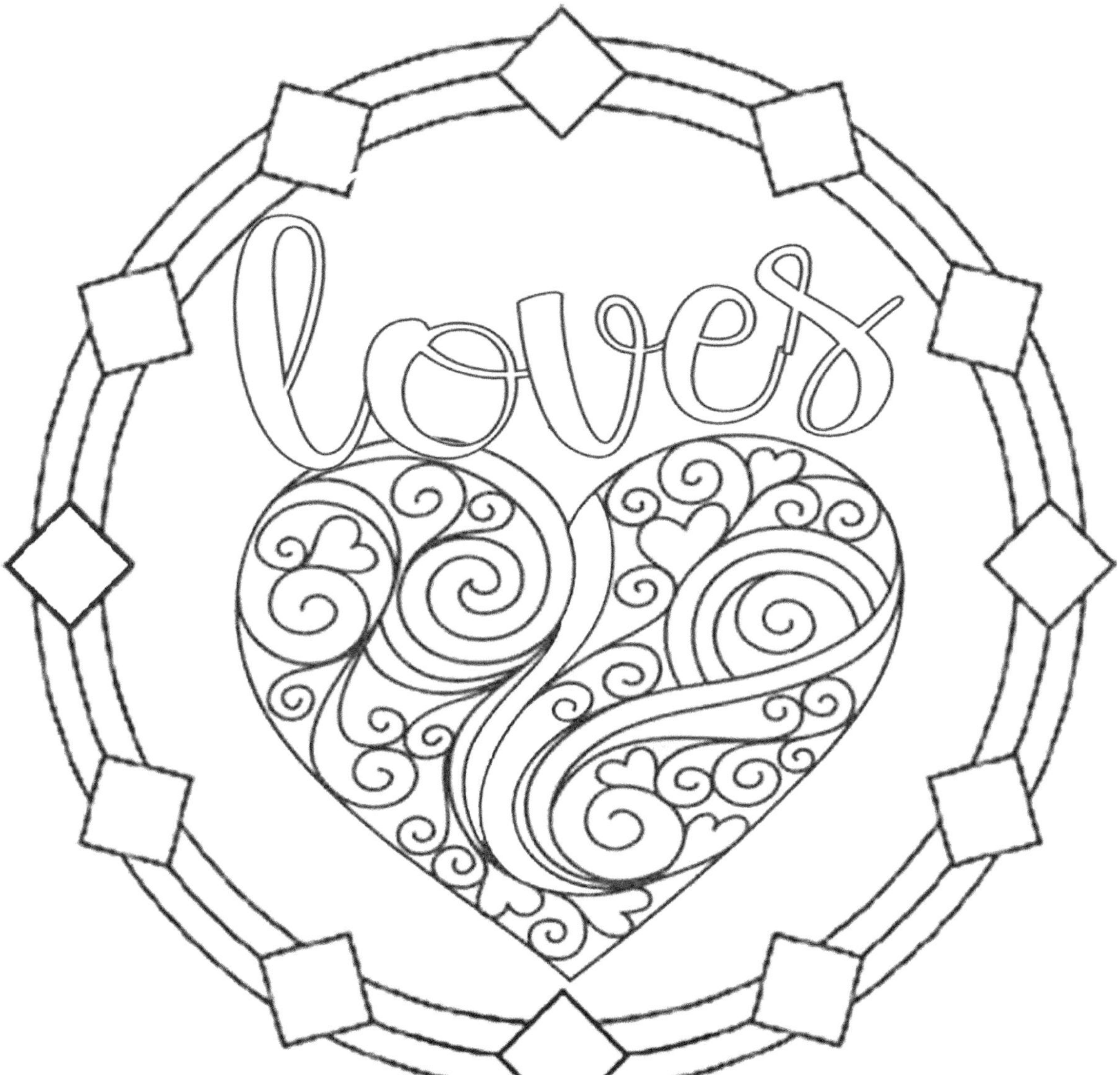
loves

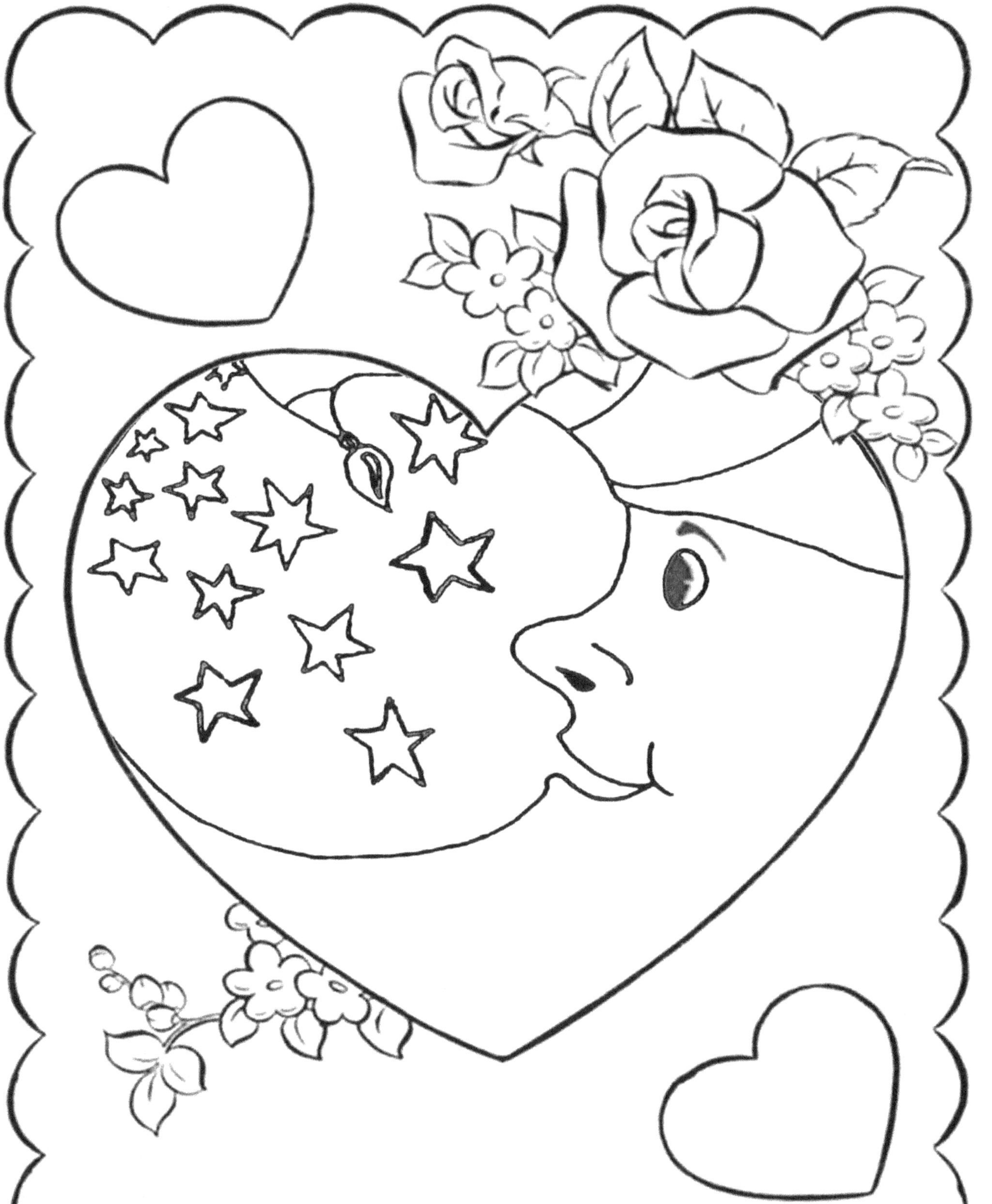

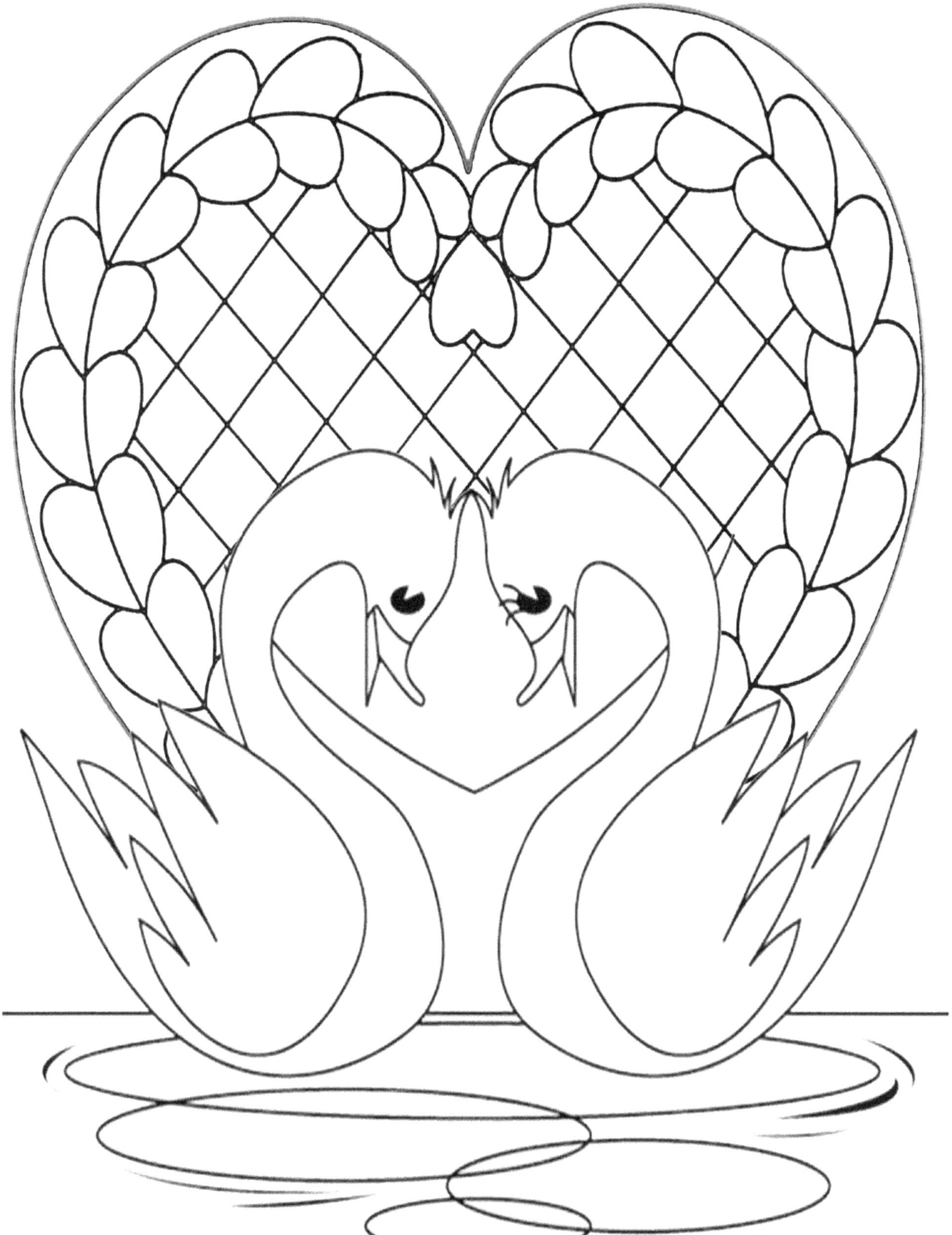

loves

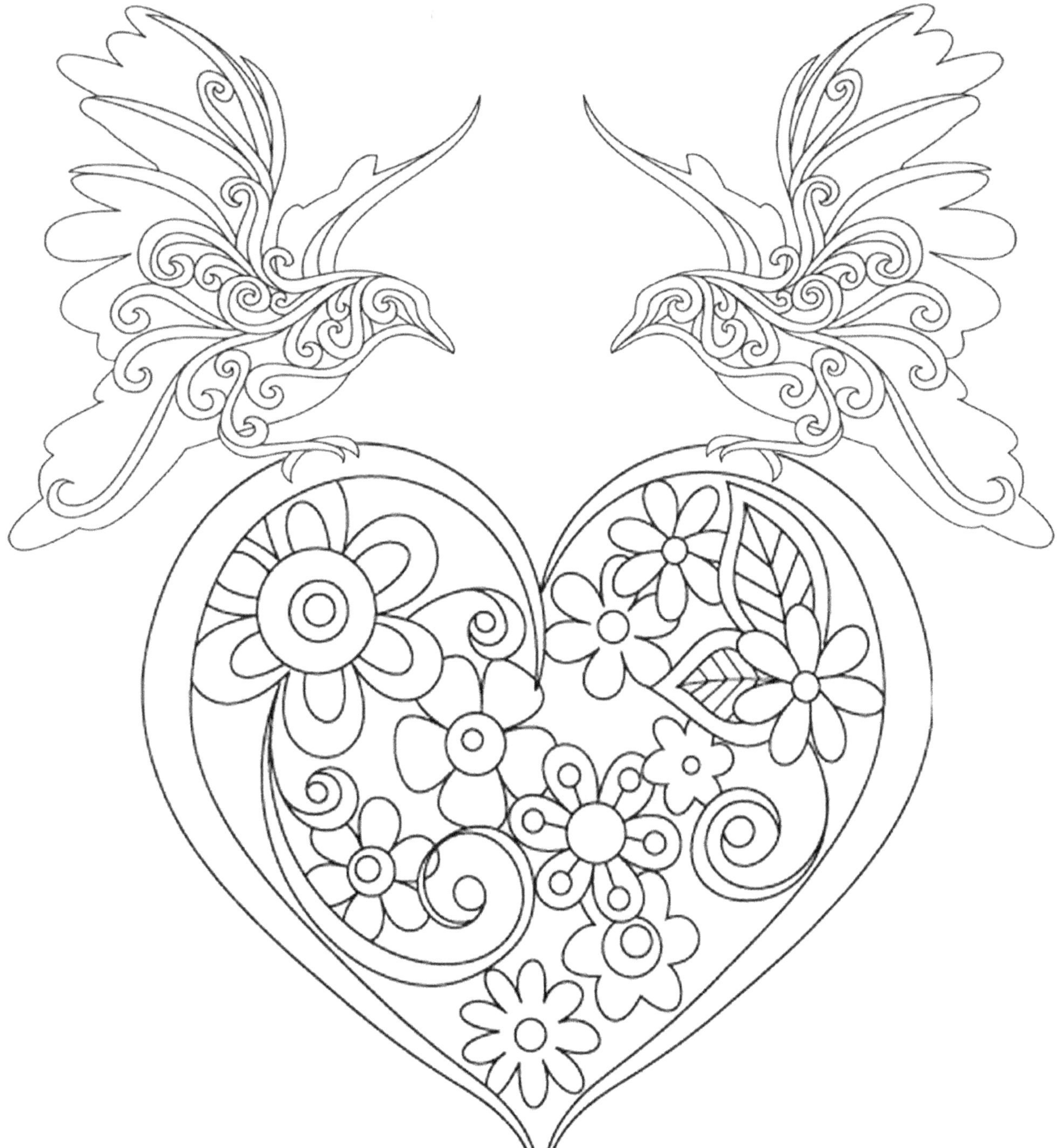

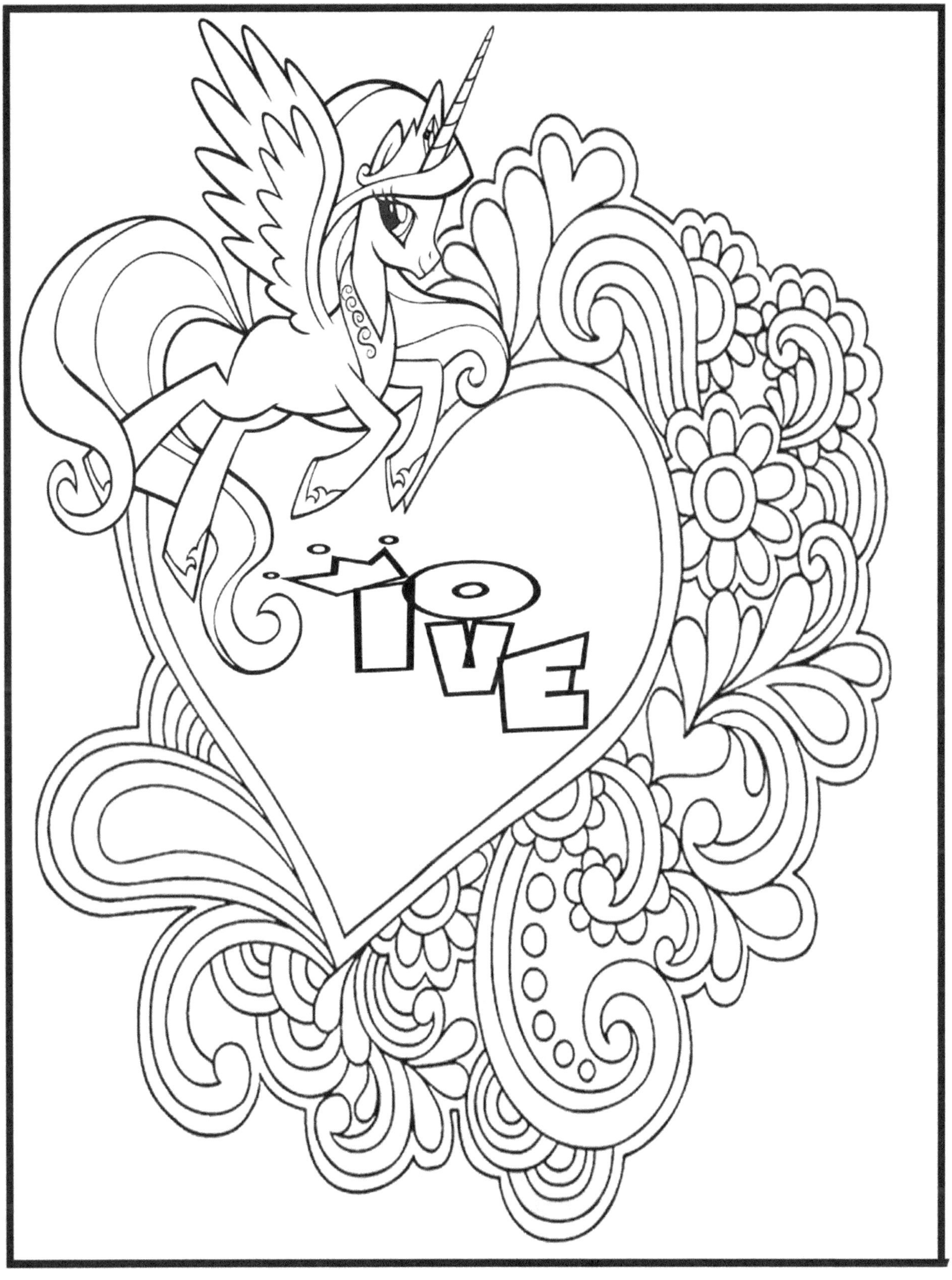

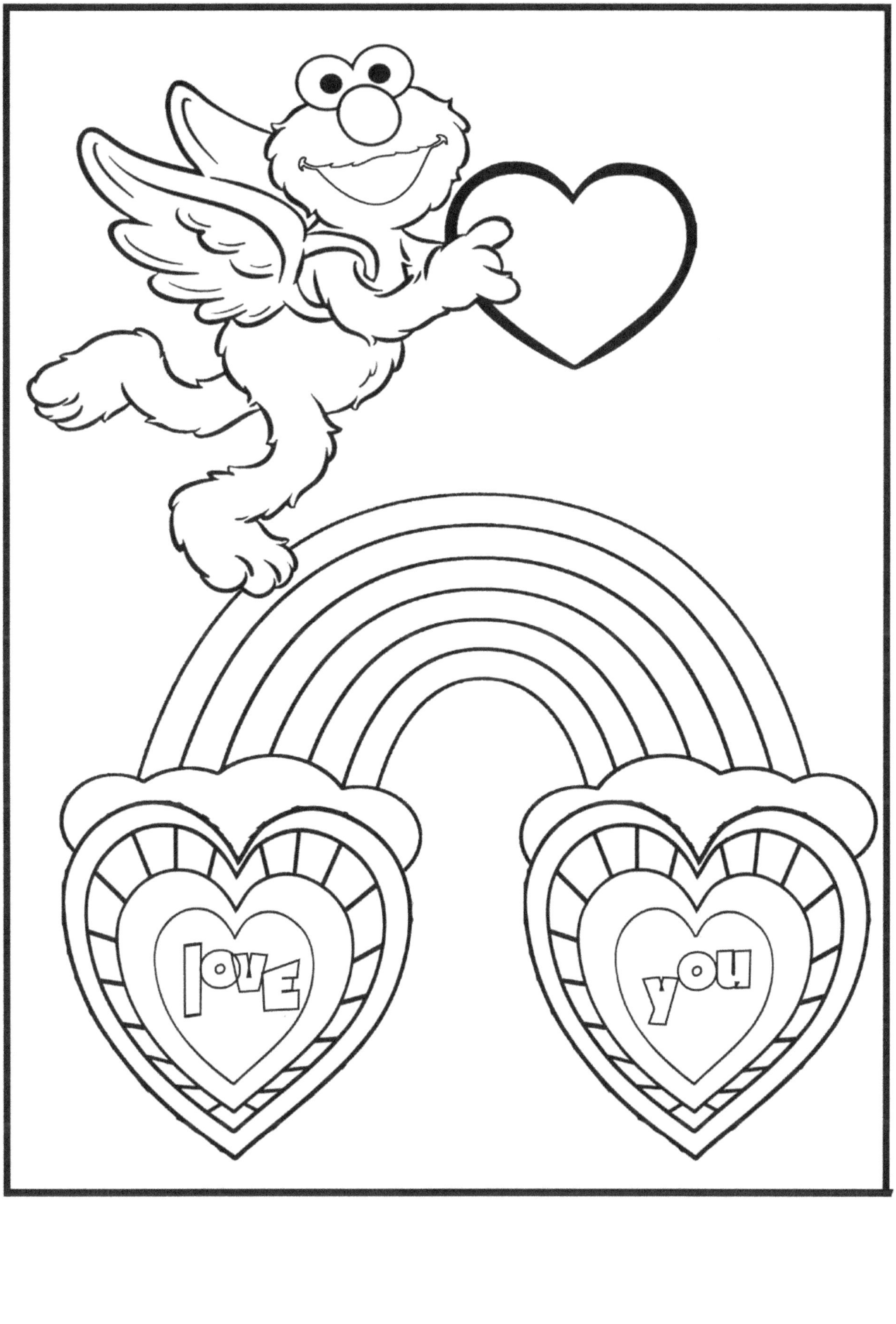
love
you

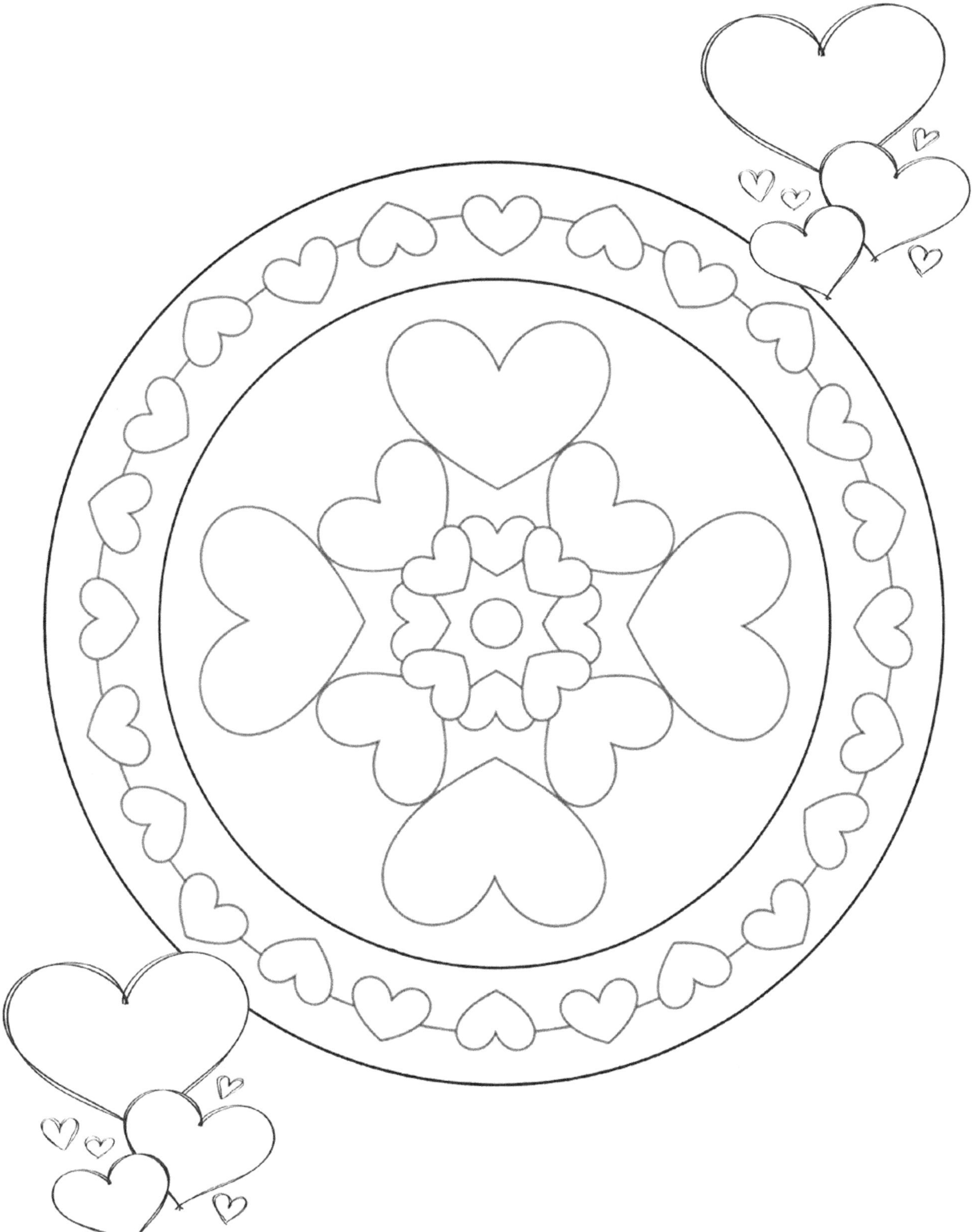

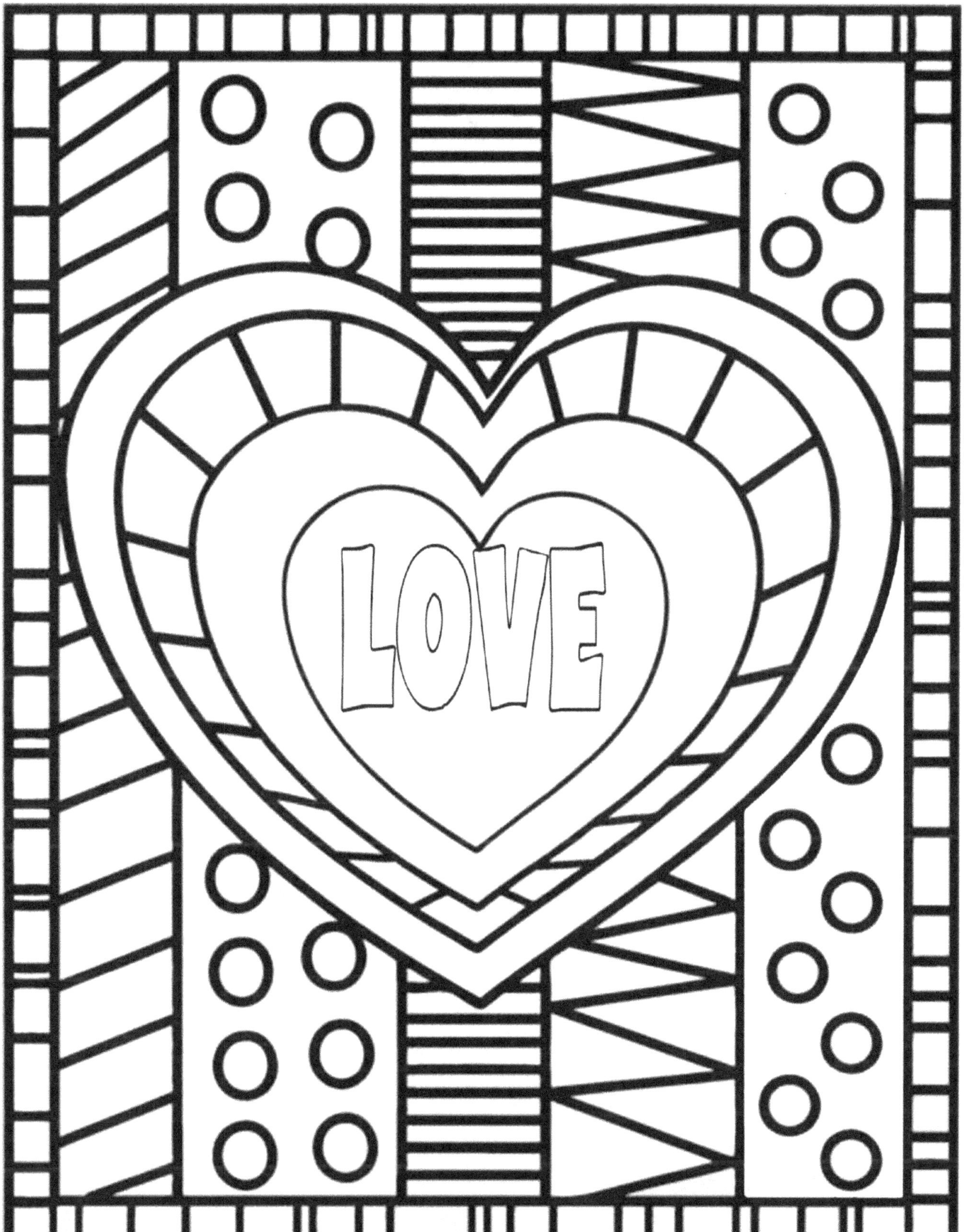
LOVE

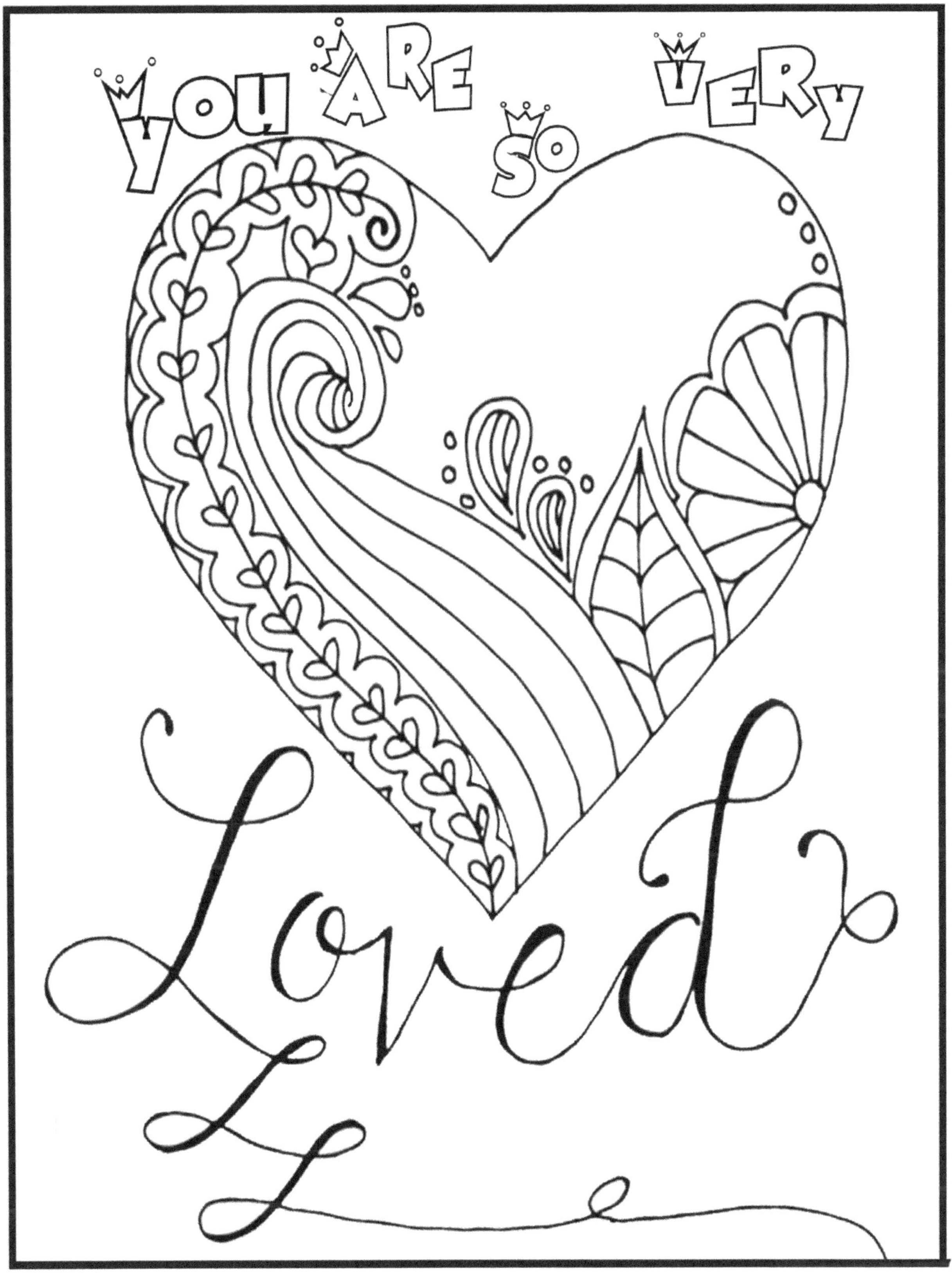
YOU ARE SO VERY
Loved

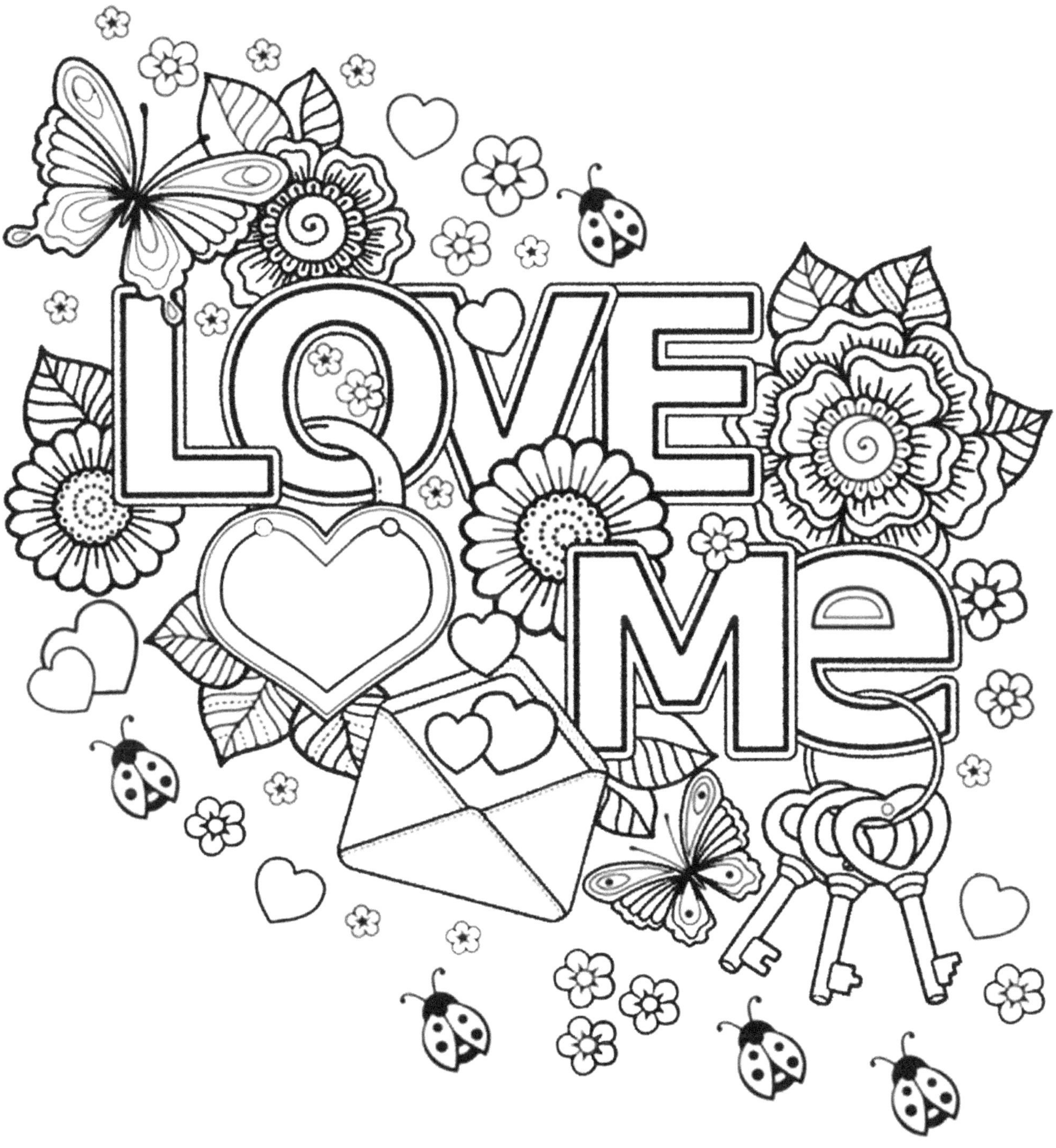
LOVE
Me

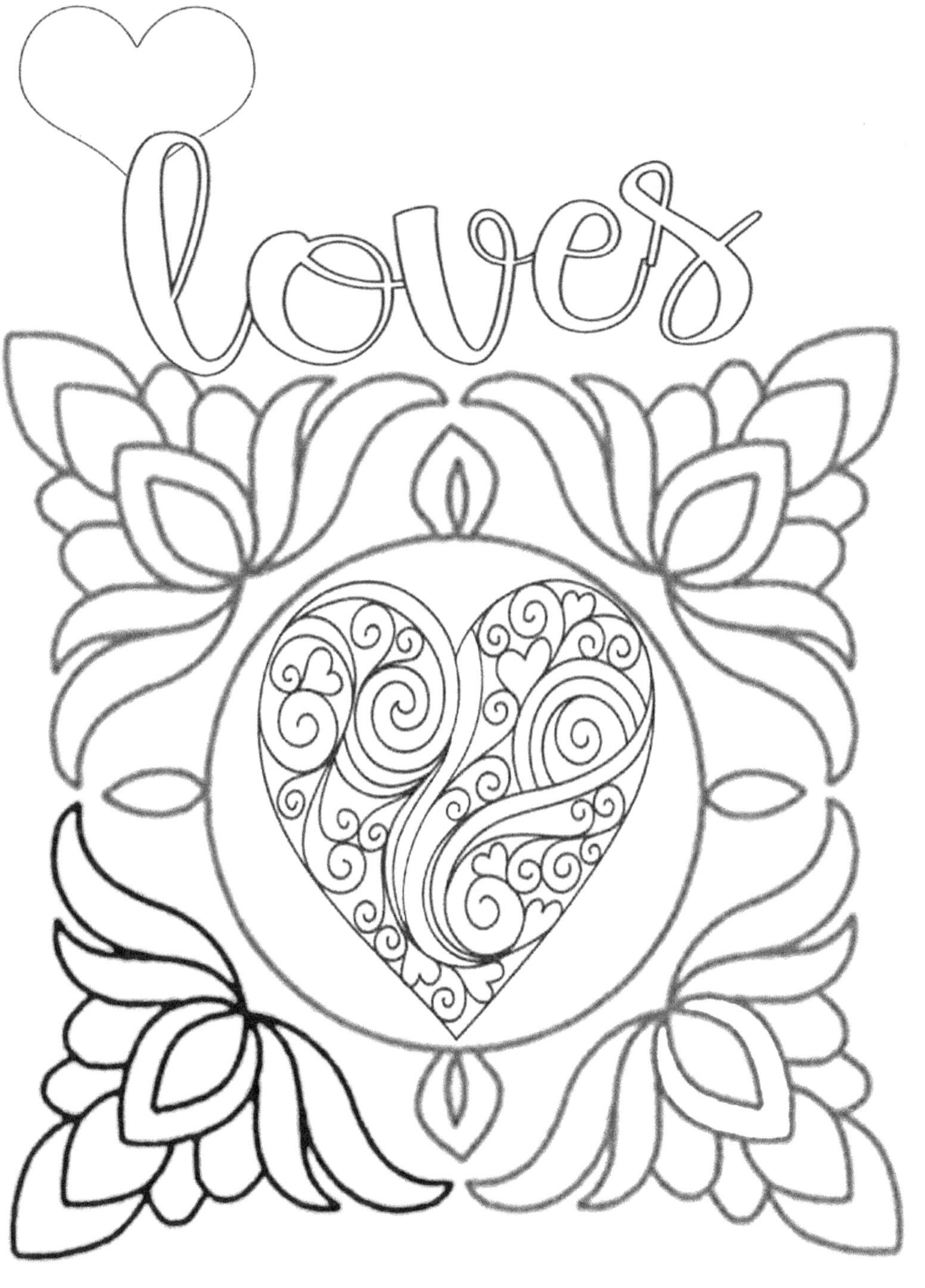
loves

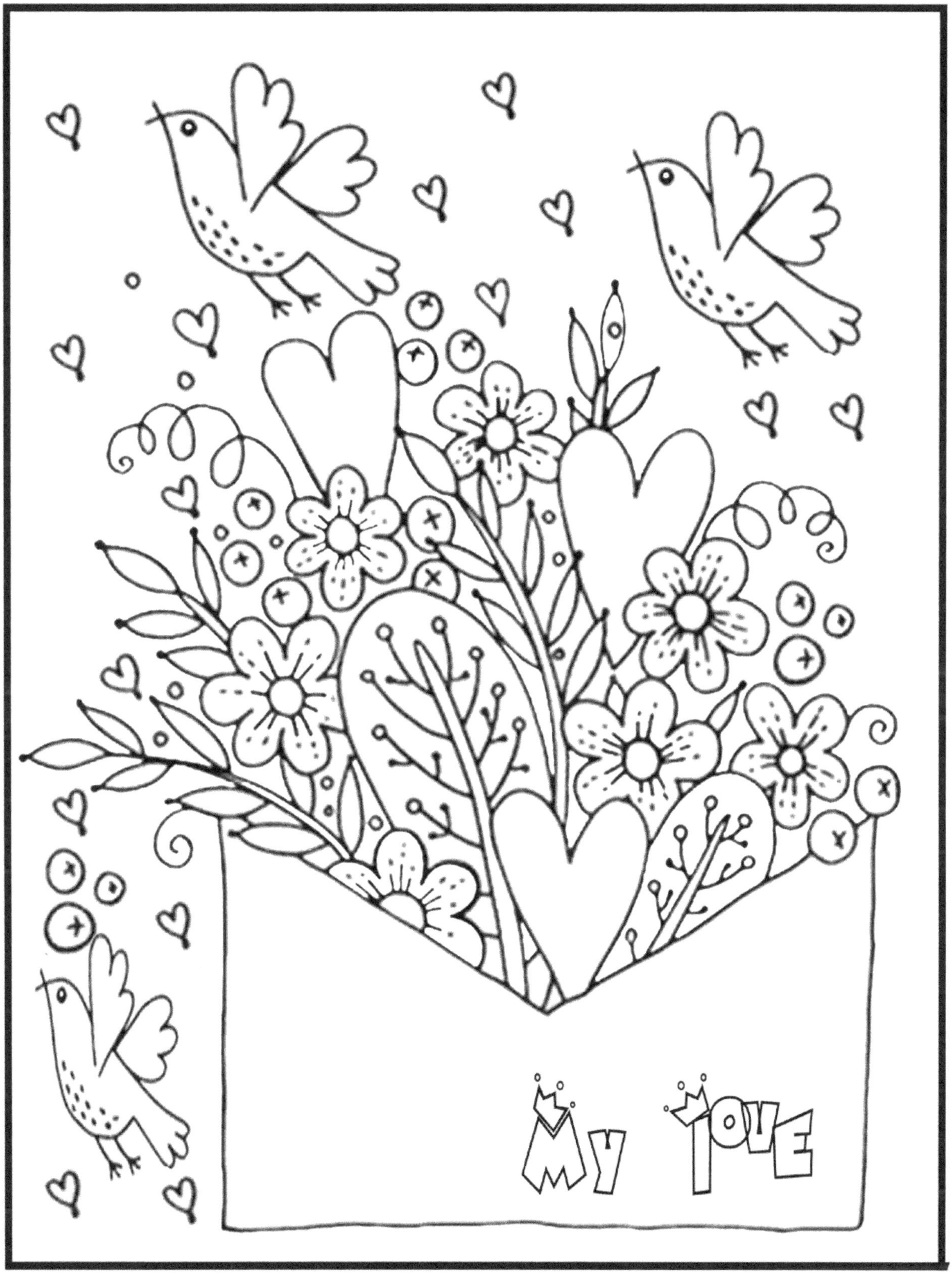
My love

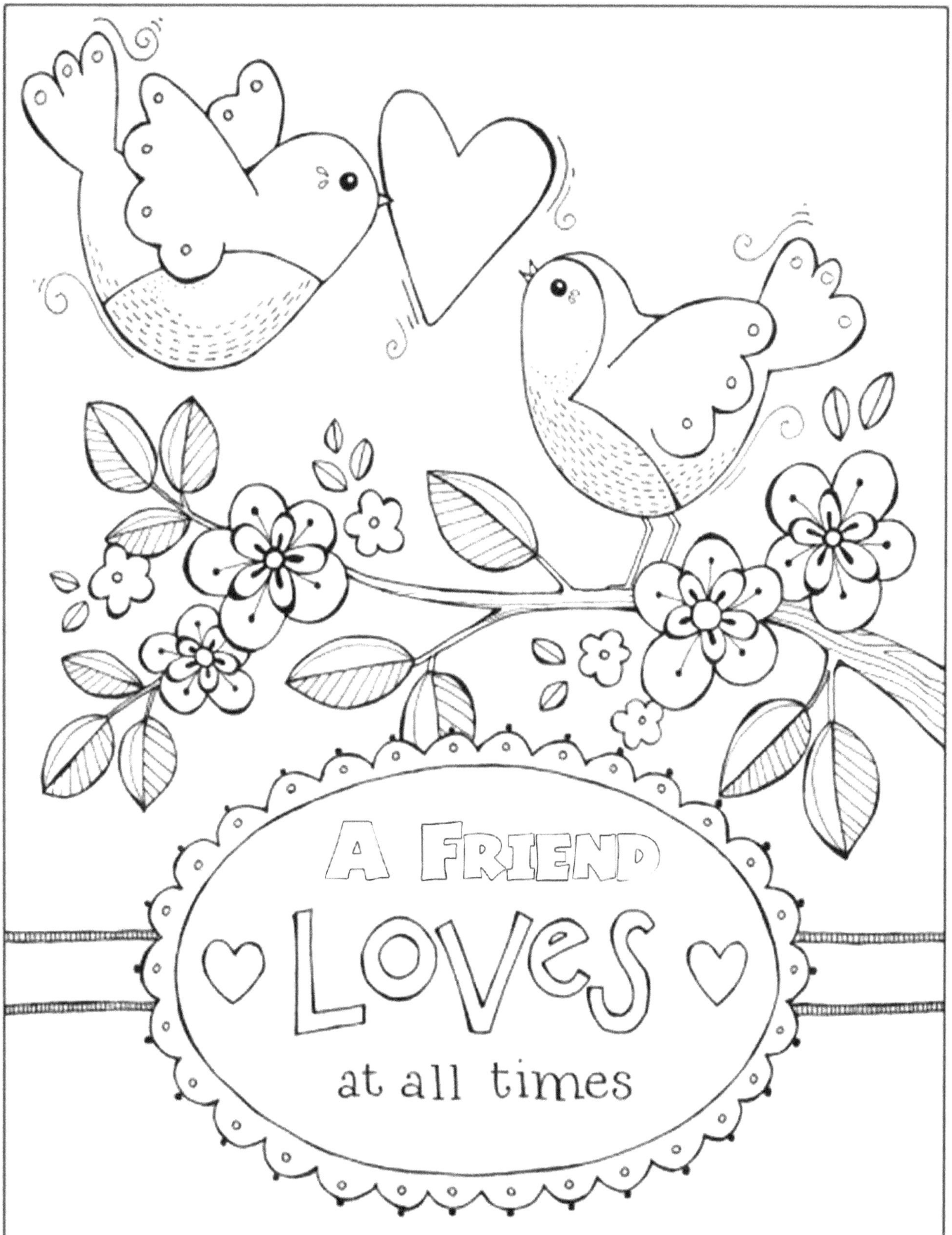
A FRIEND
LOVES
at all times

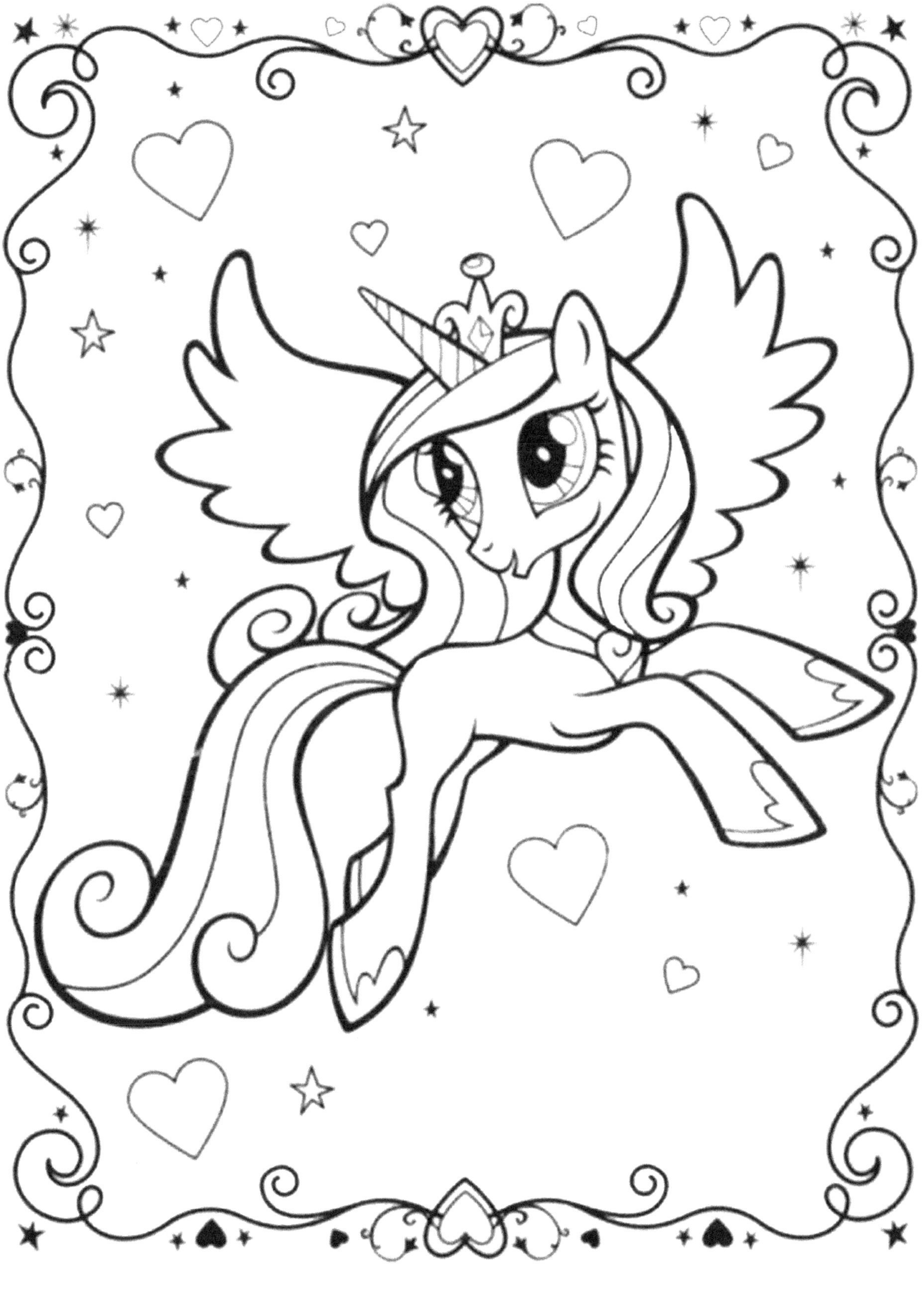

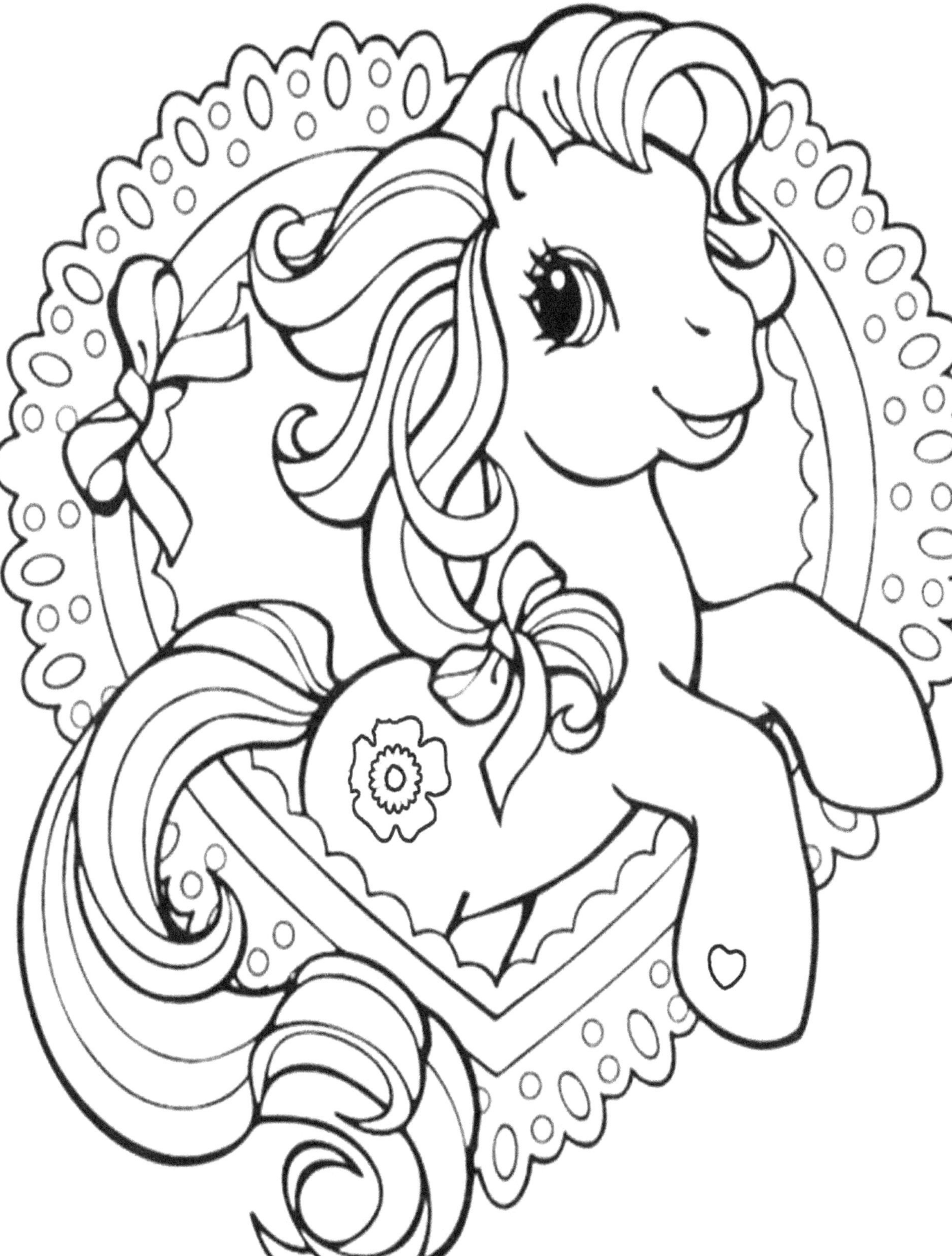

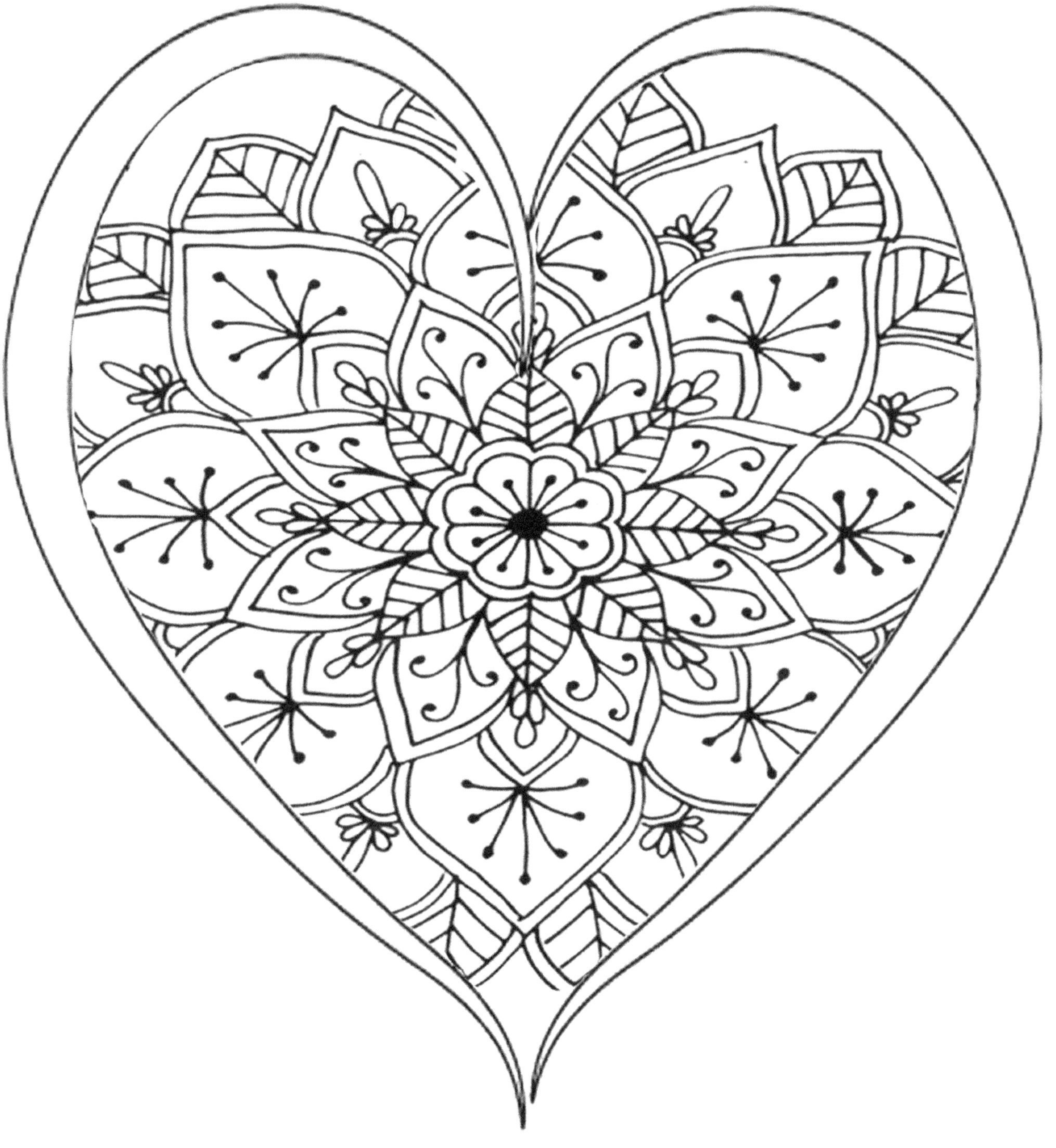

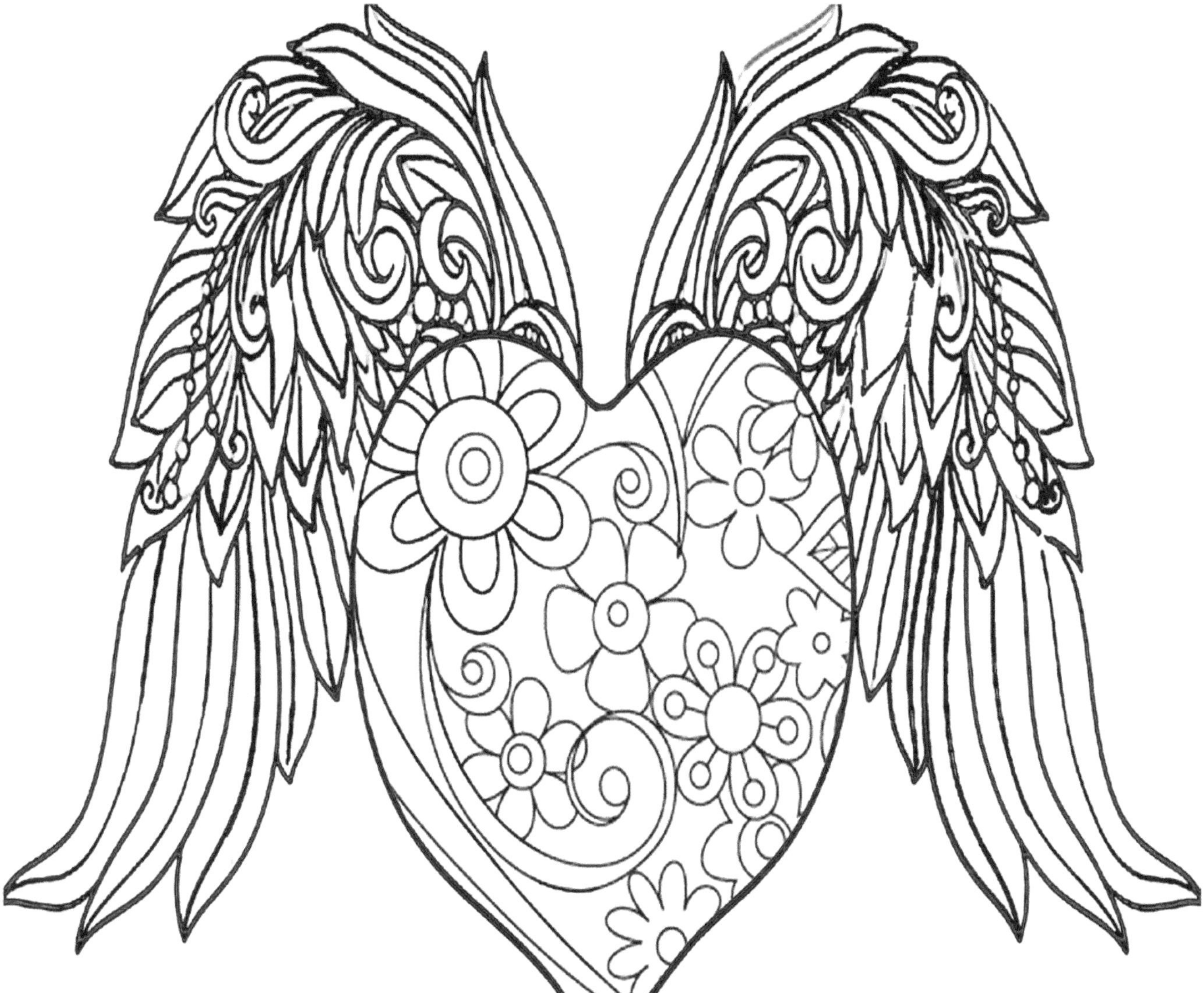

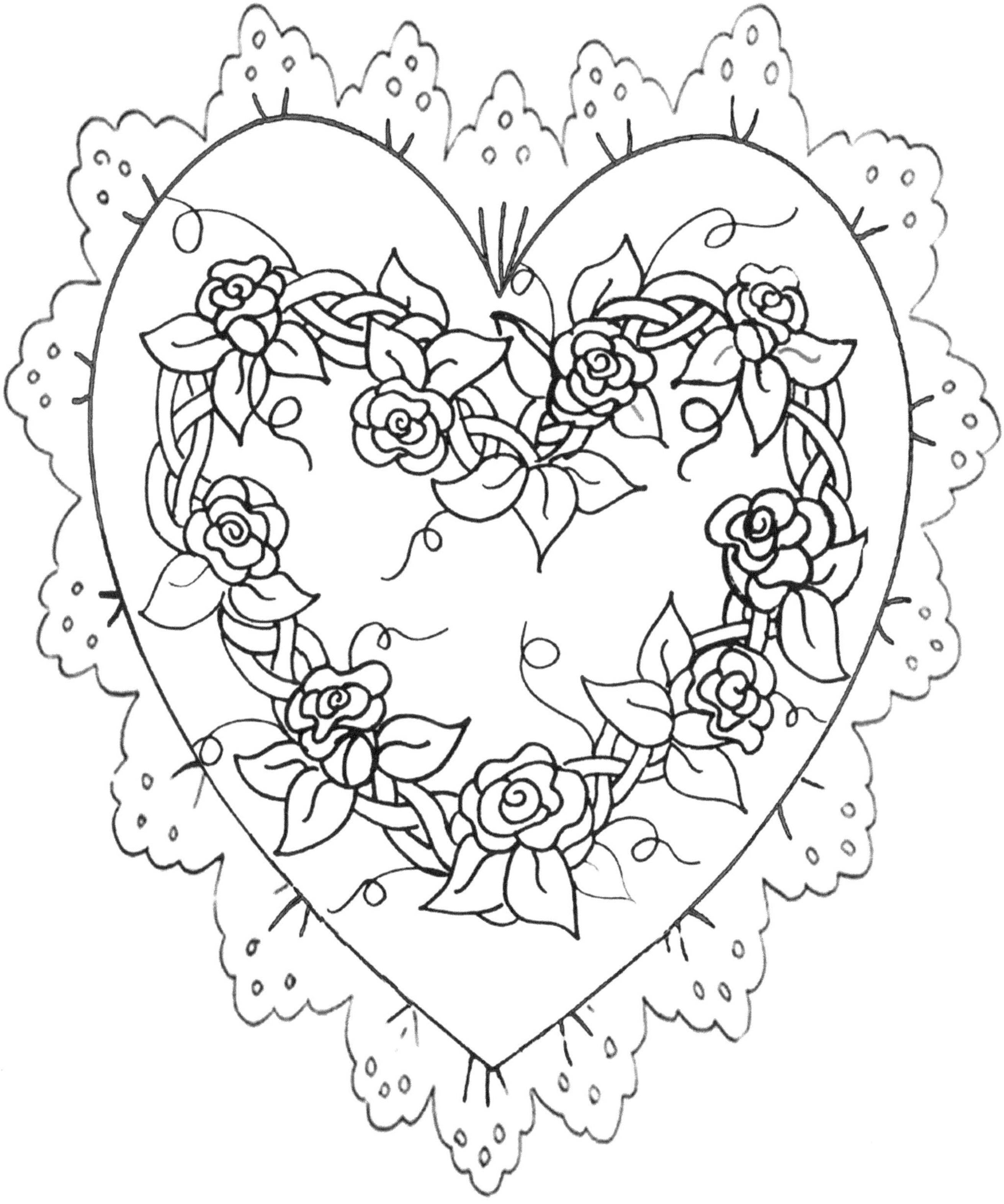

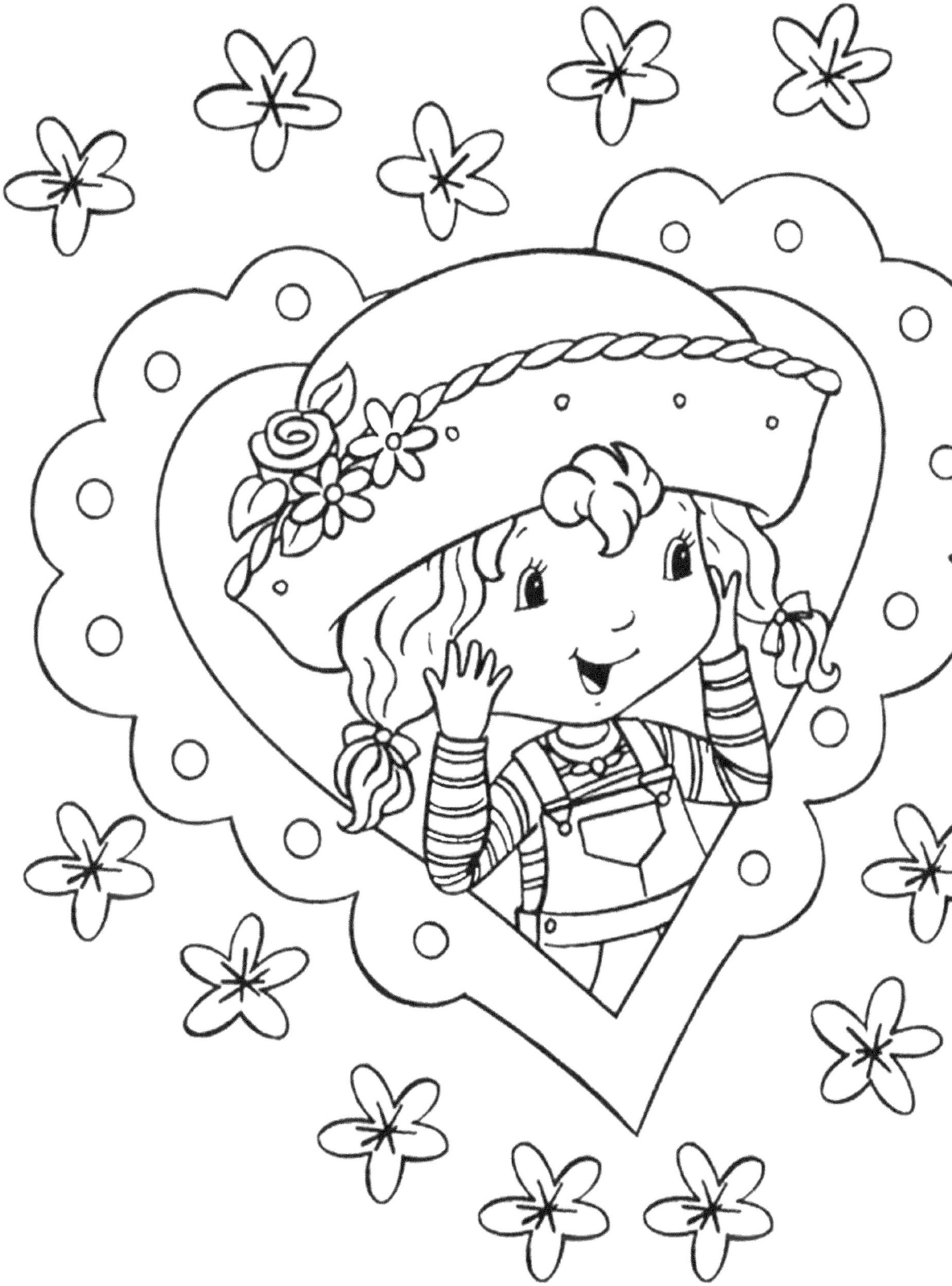

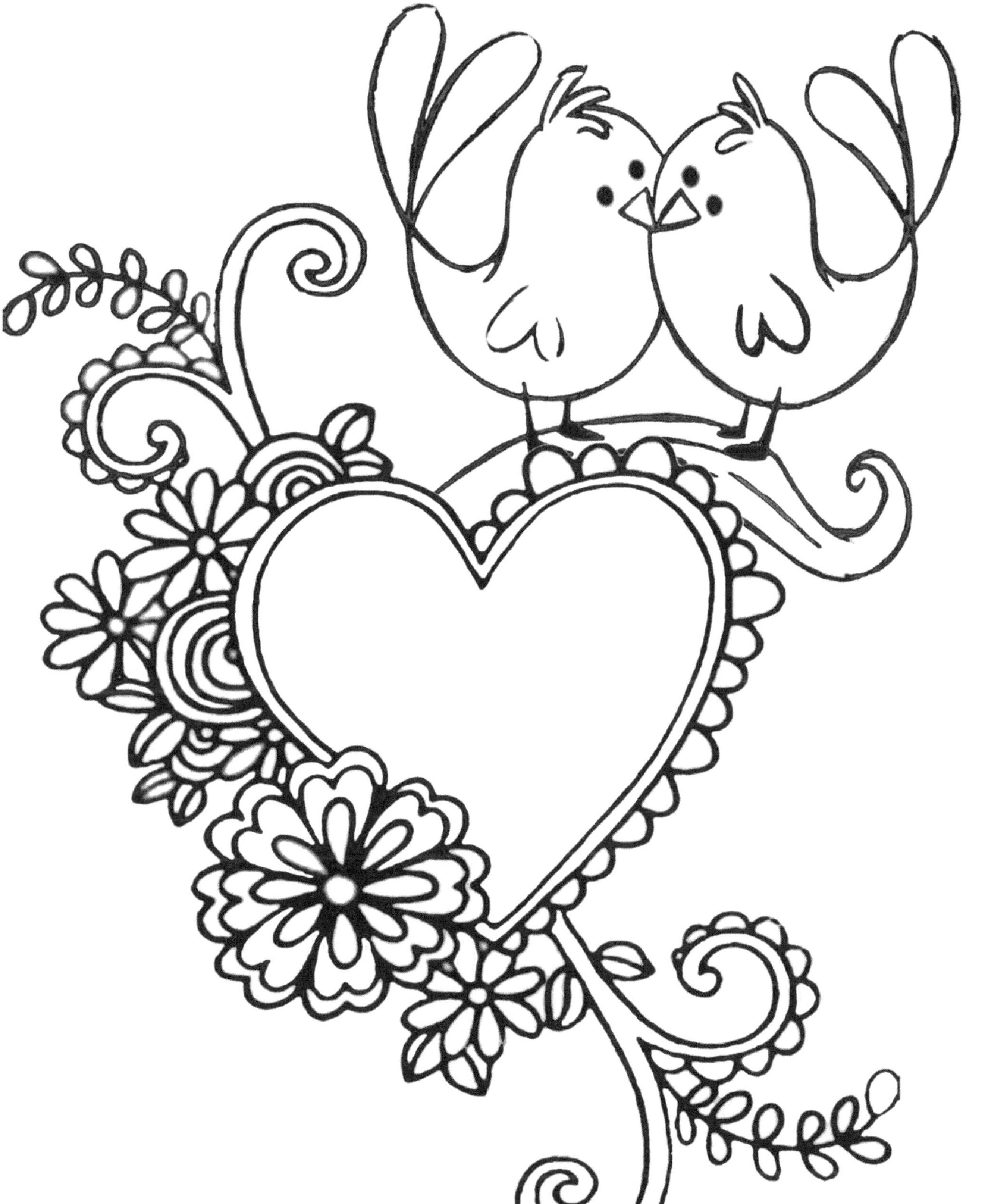

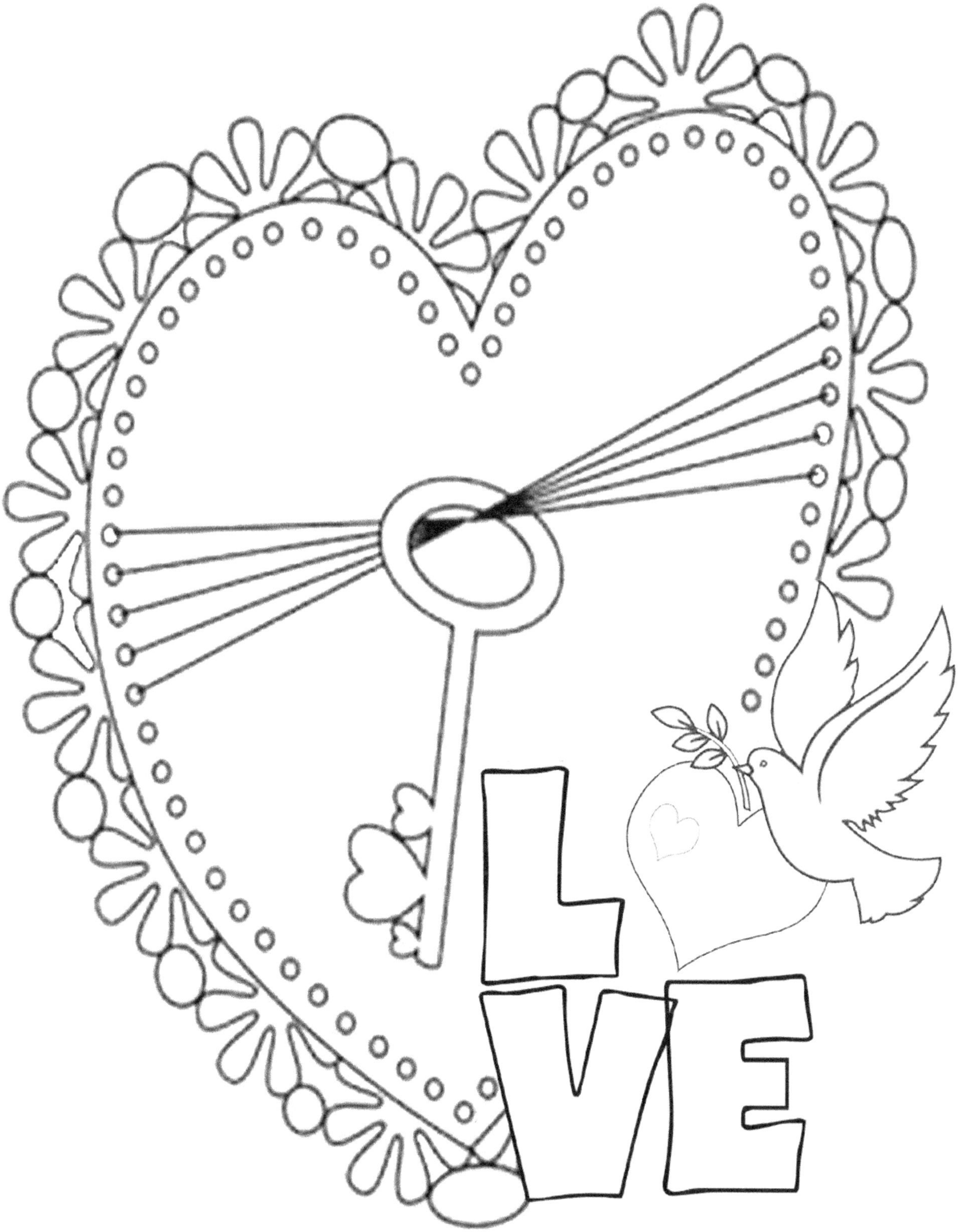
LOVE

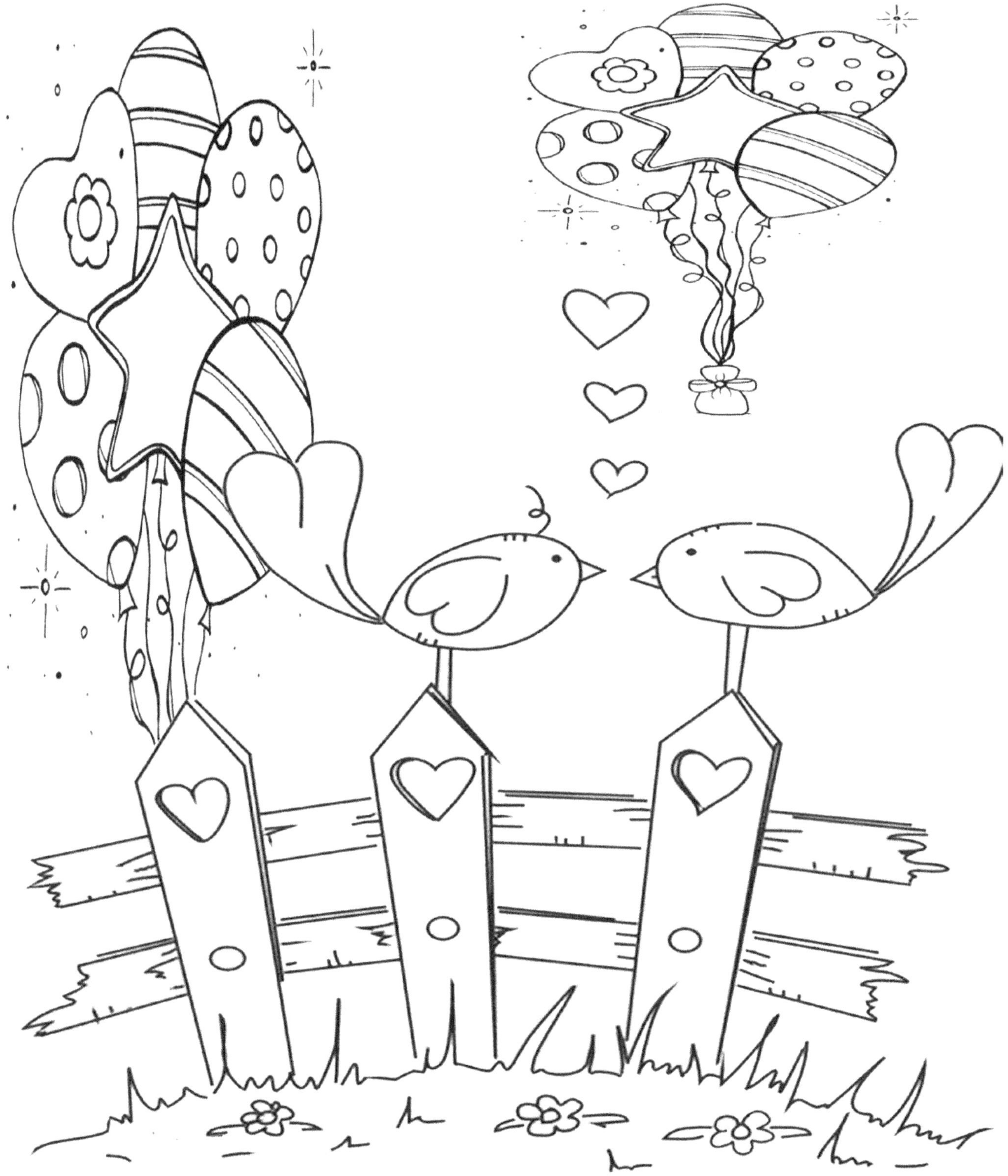

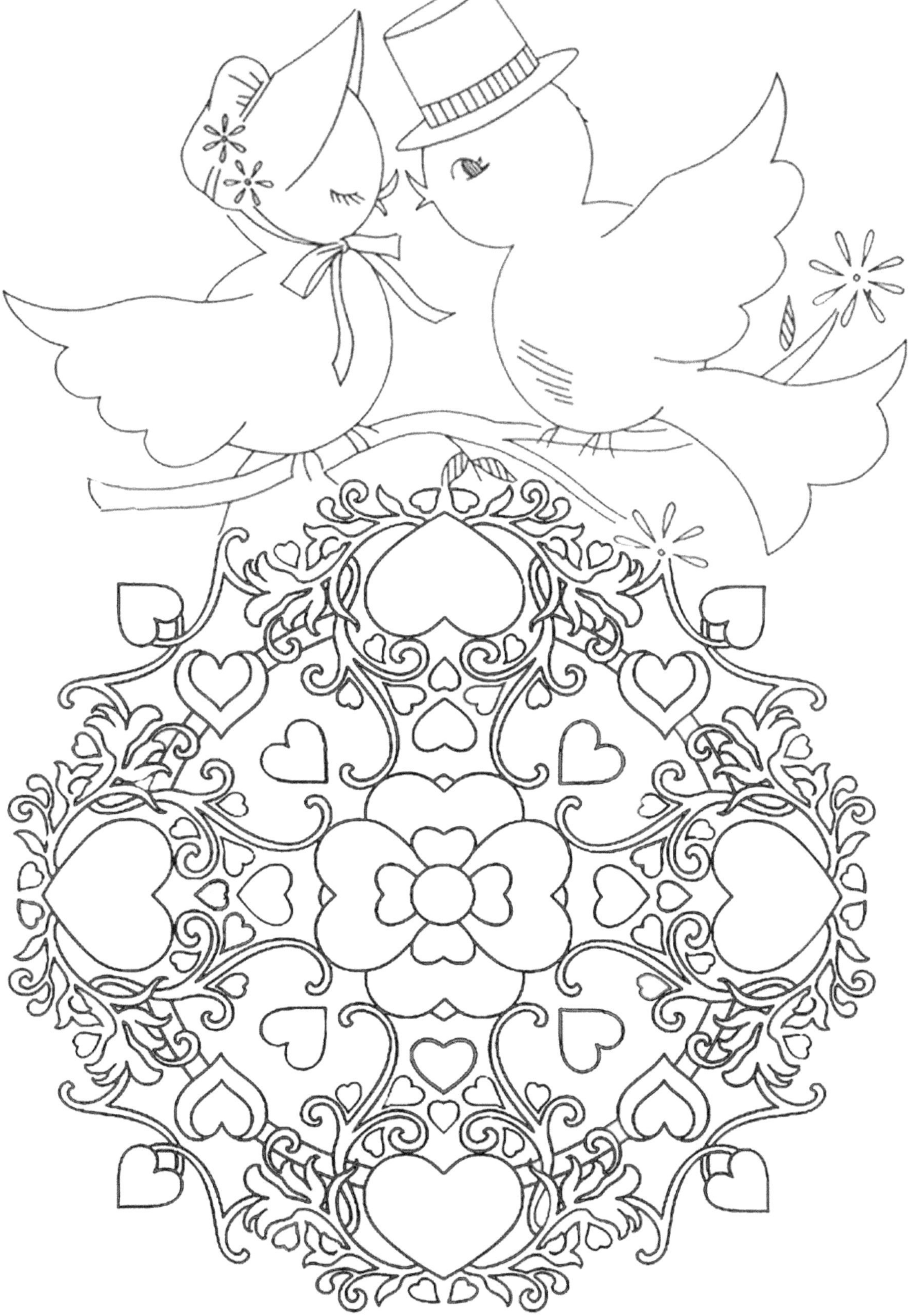

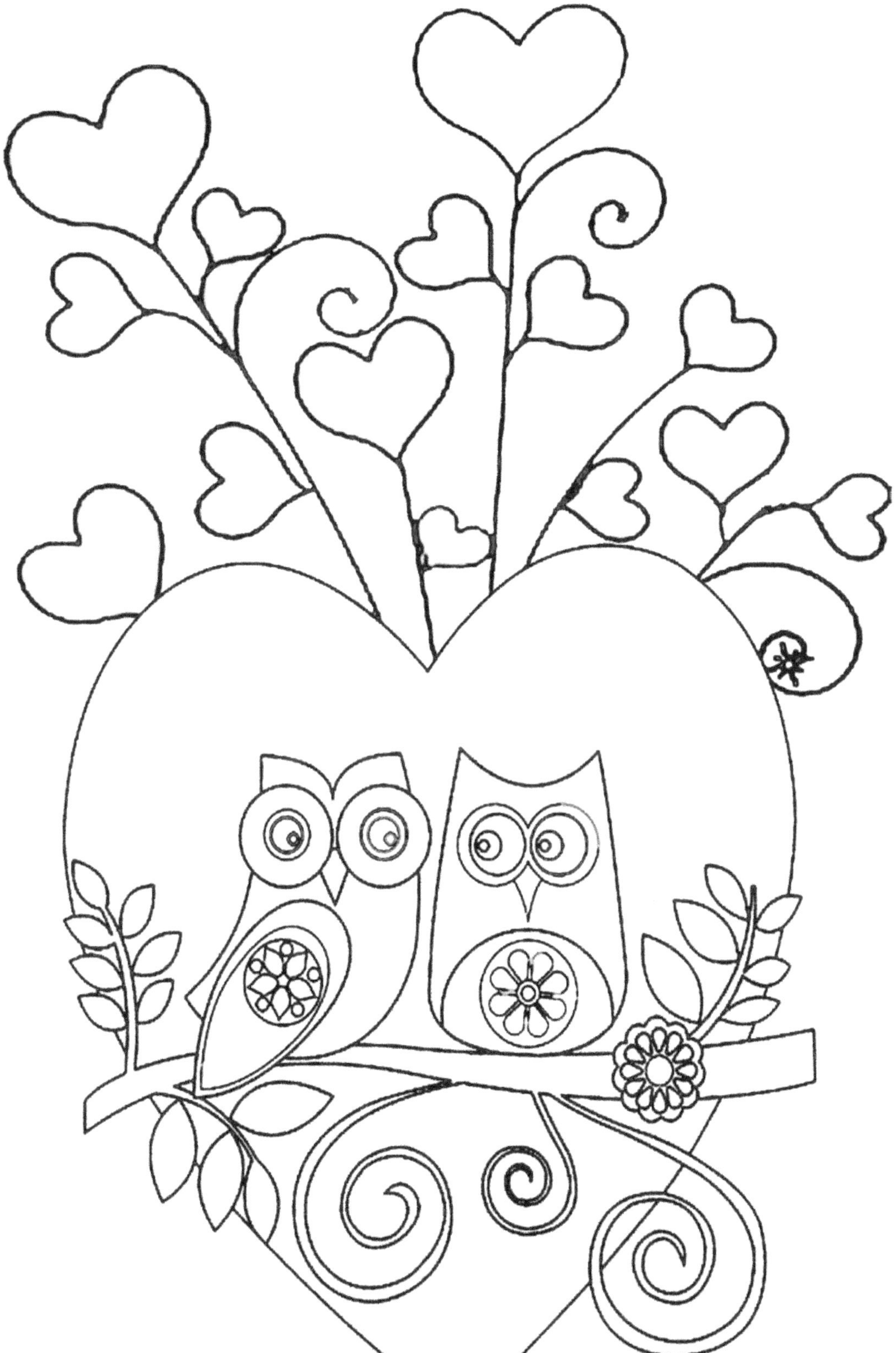

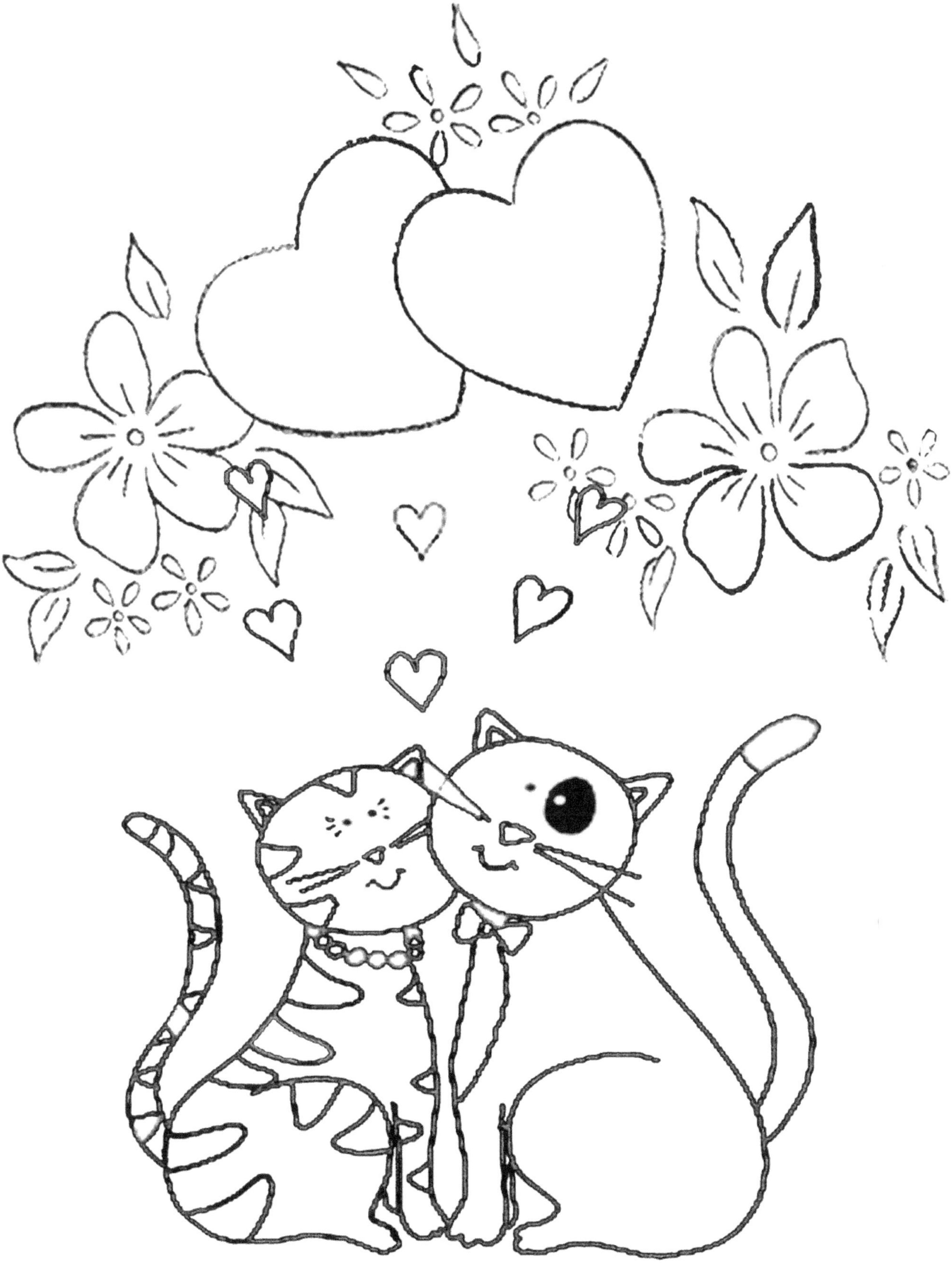

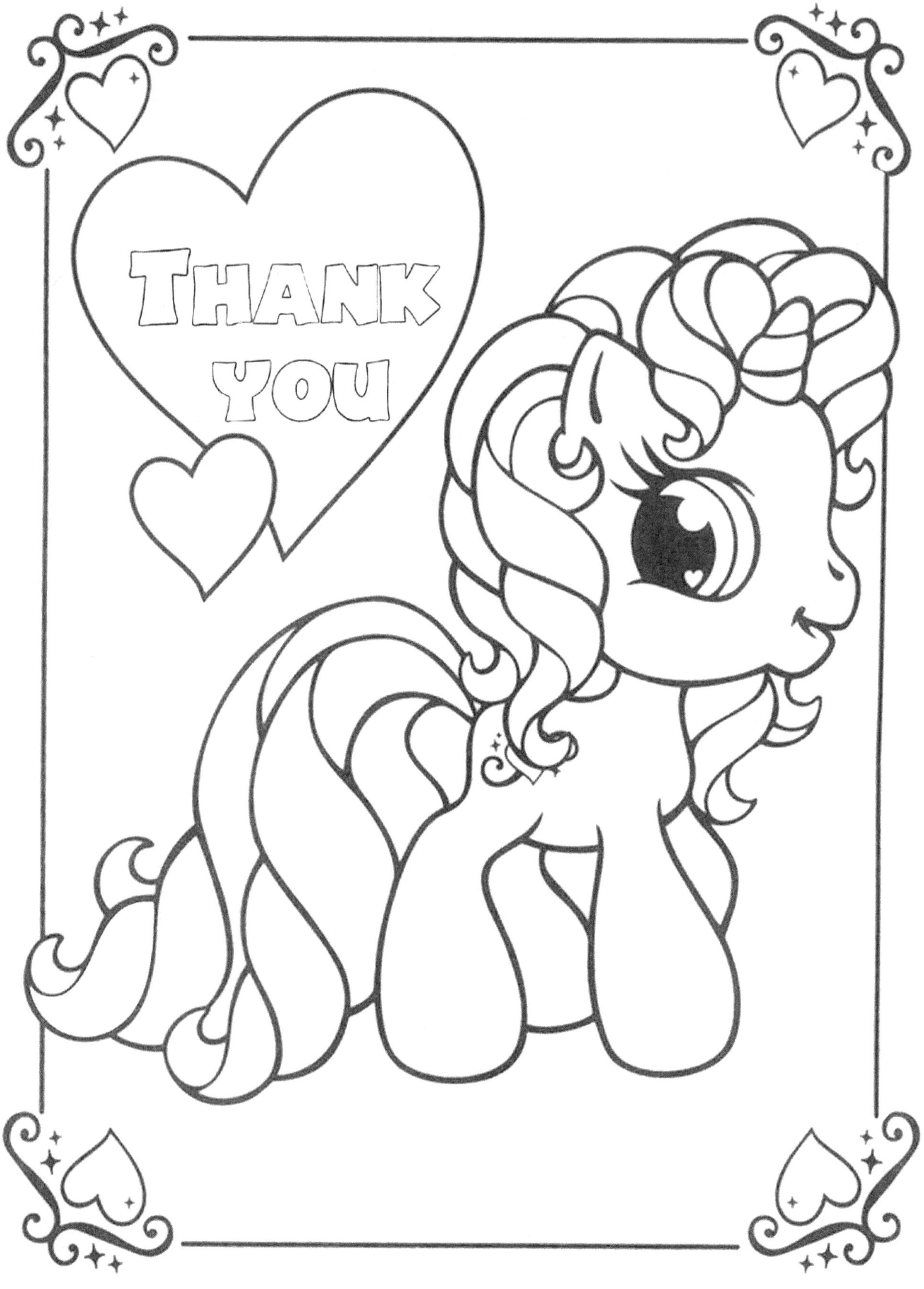
THANK YOU

www.ingramcontent.com/pod-product-compliance
Lightning Source LLC
Chambersburg PA
CBHW081616220526
45468CB00010B/2903
* 9 7 8 1 9 8 3 7 0 7 7 7 3 *